Coloring Book for Kids

COLORING
BOOK FOR KIDS
COOL CARS AND TRUCKS

Illustrations by Collaborate Agency

ROCKRIDGE
PRESS

For general information on our other products and services or to obtain technical support, please contact our Customer Care Department within the U.S. at (866) 744-2665, or outside the U.S. at (510) 253-0500.

Rockridge Press publishes its books in a variety of electronic and print formats. Some content that appears in print may not be available in electronic books, and vice versa.

TRADEMARKS: Rockridge Press and the Rockridge Press logo are trademarks or registered trademarks of Callisto Media Inc. and/or its affiliates, in the United States and other countries, and may not be used without written permission. All other trademarks are the property of their respective owners. Rockridge Press is not associated with any product or vendor mentioned in this book.

Interior and Cover Designer: Stephanie Sumulong
Art Producer: Megan Baggott
Editor: Alyson Penn
Production Editor: Mia Moran
Production Manager: Jose Olivera

Illustrations © 2021 Collaborate Agency

Paperback ISBN: 978-1-63807-940-8
R0

Coloring Test Page

Test your markers, crayons, or colored pencils
on this page before you begin.

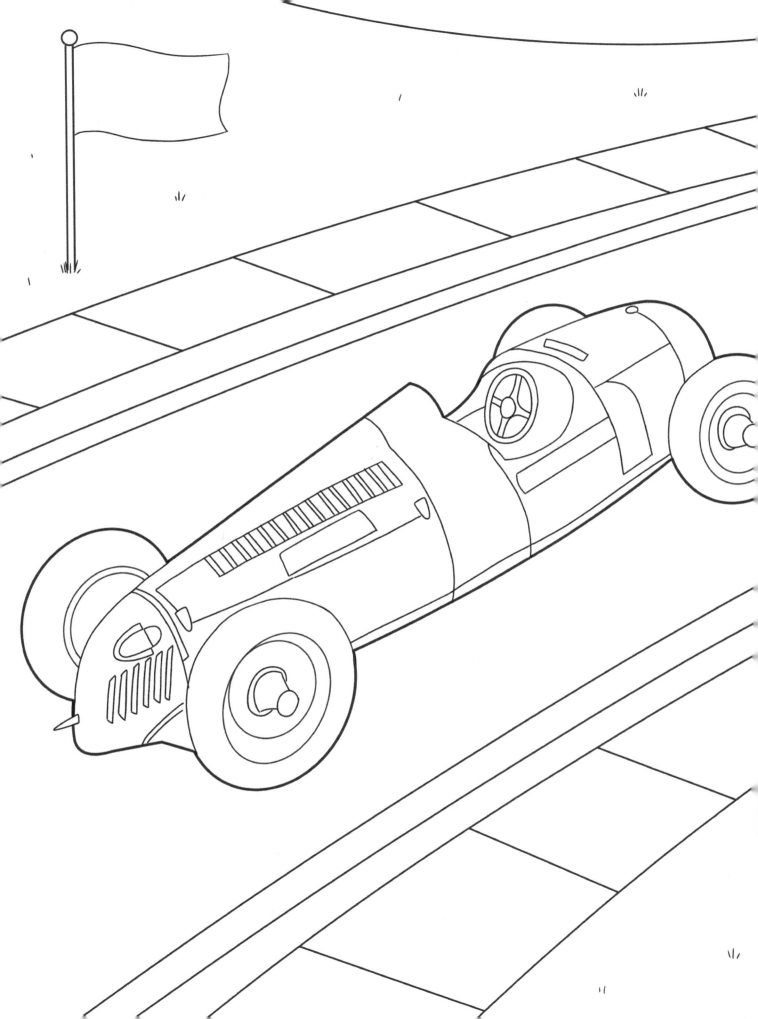

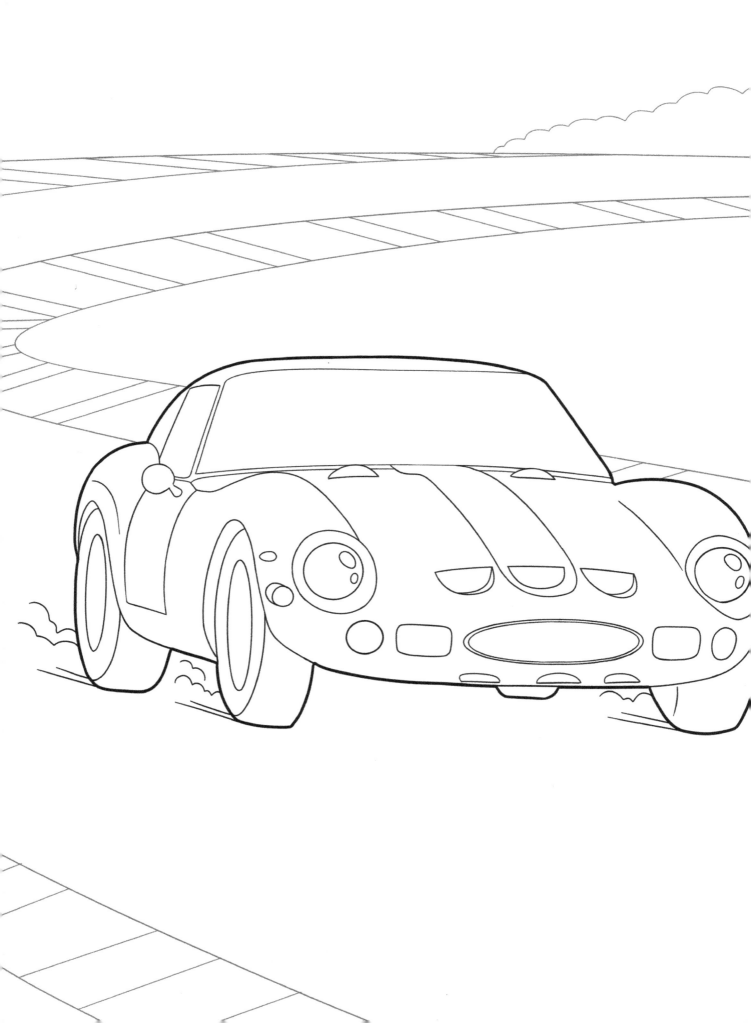

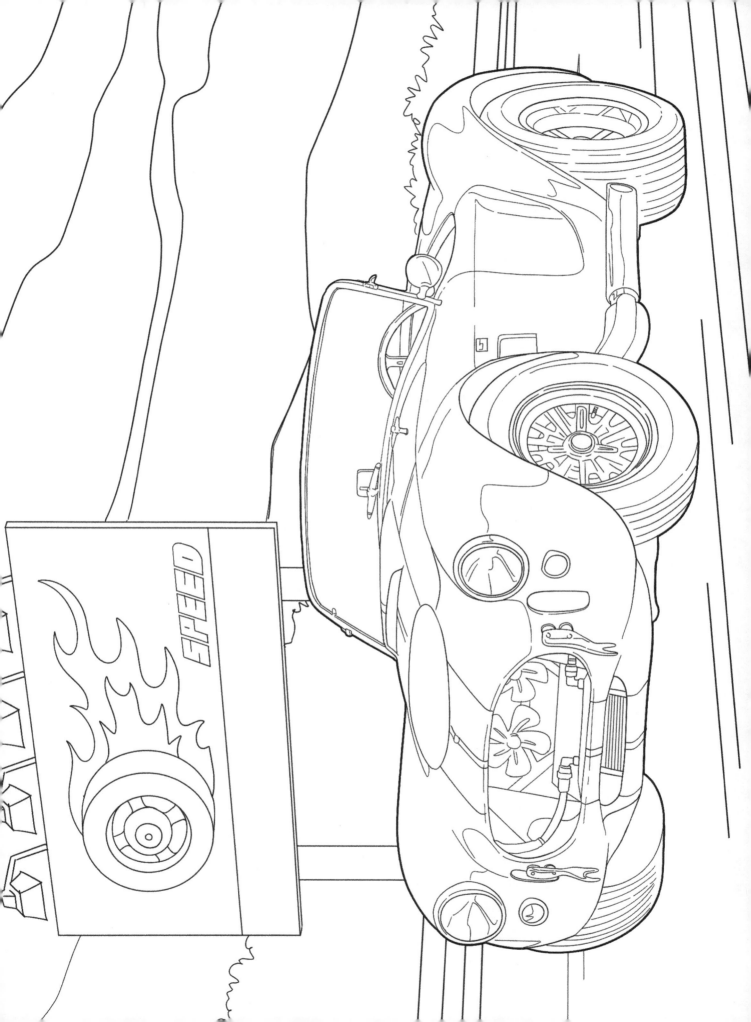

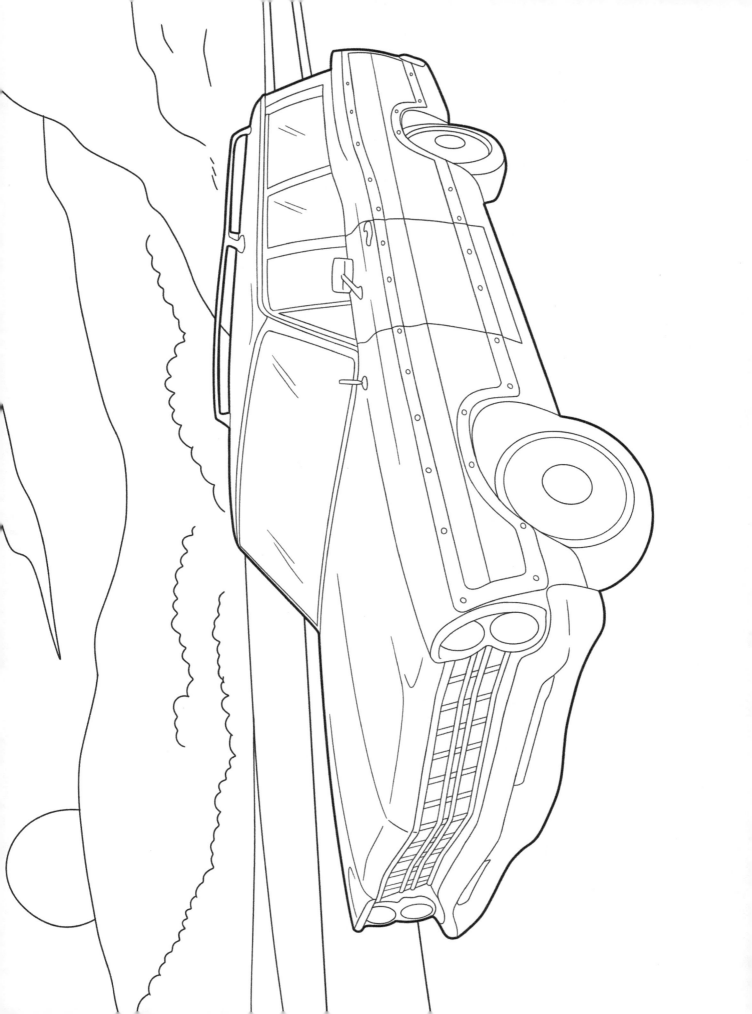

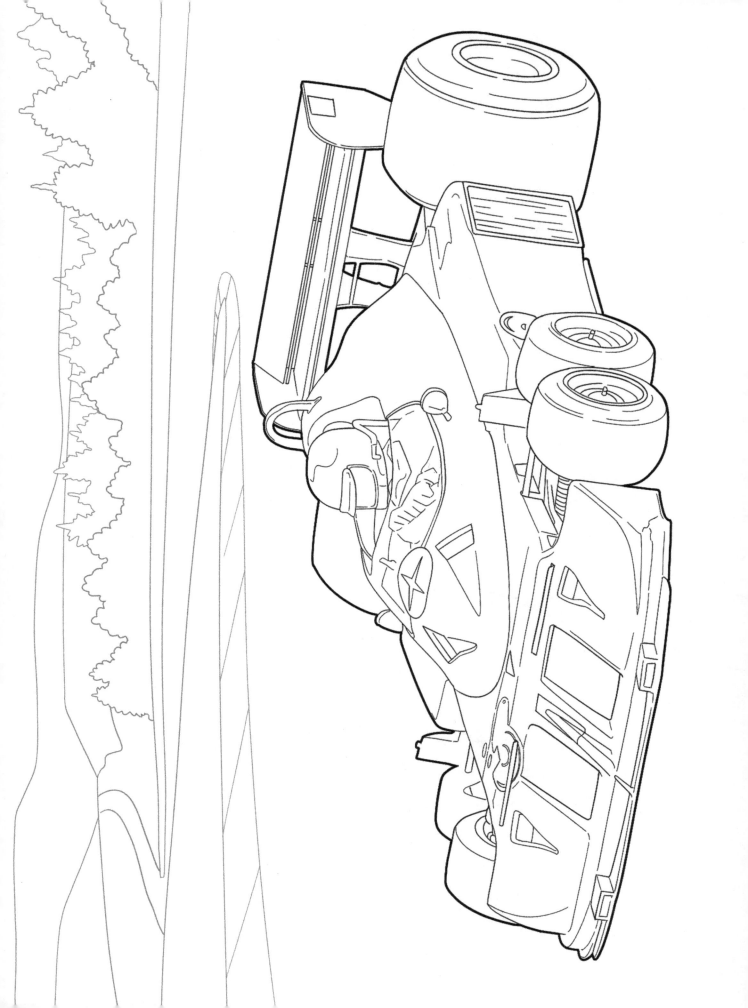

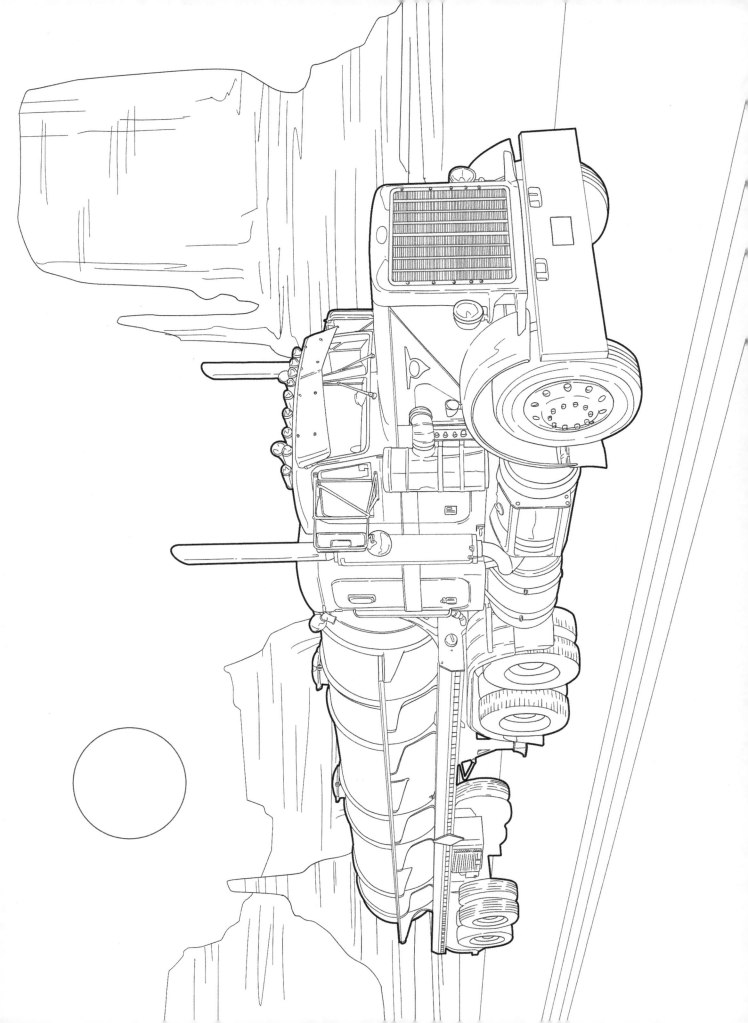

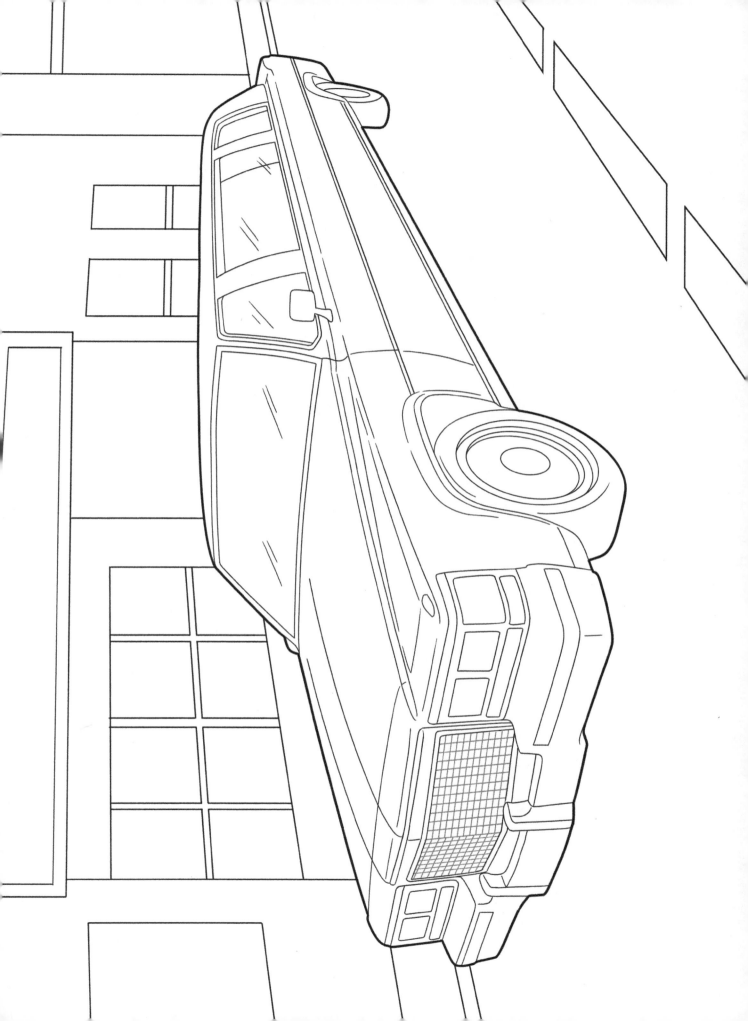

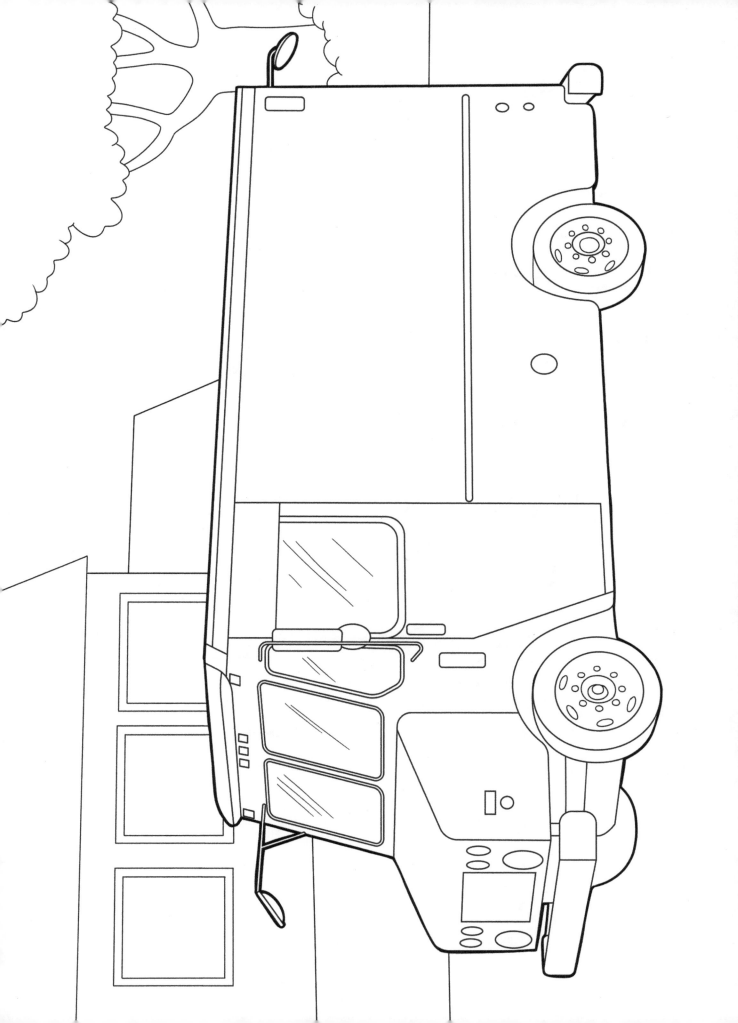

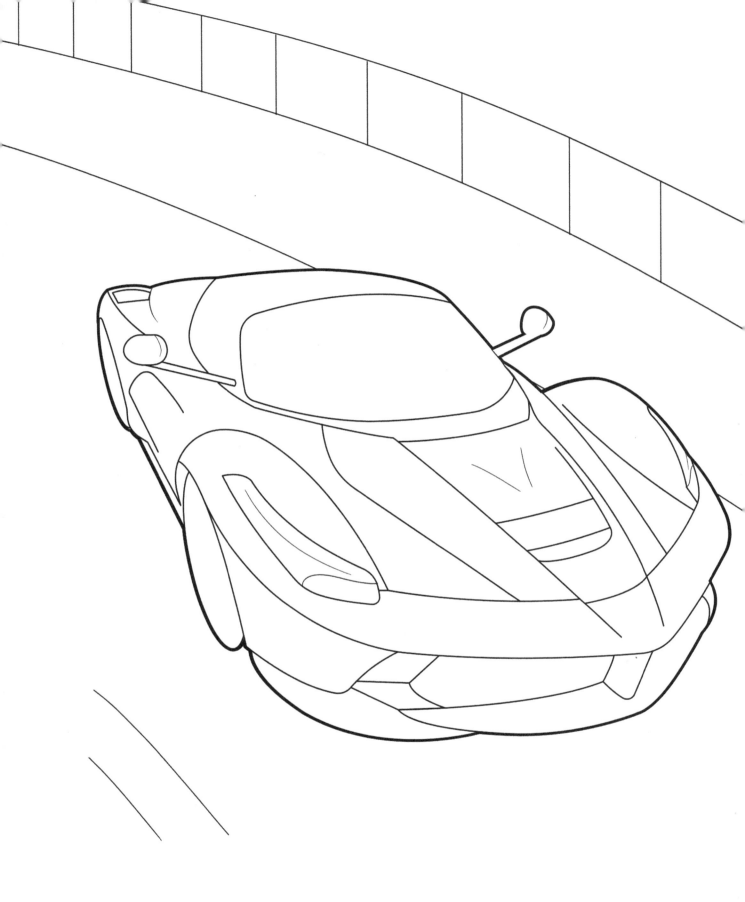

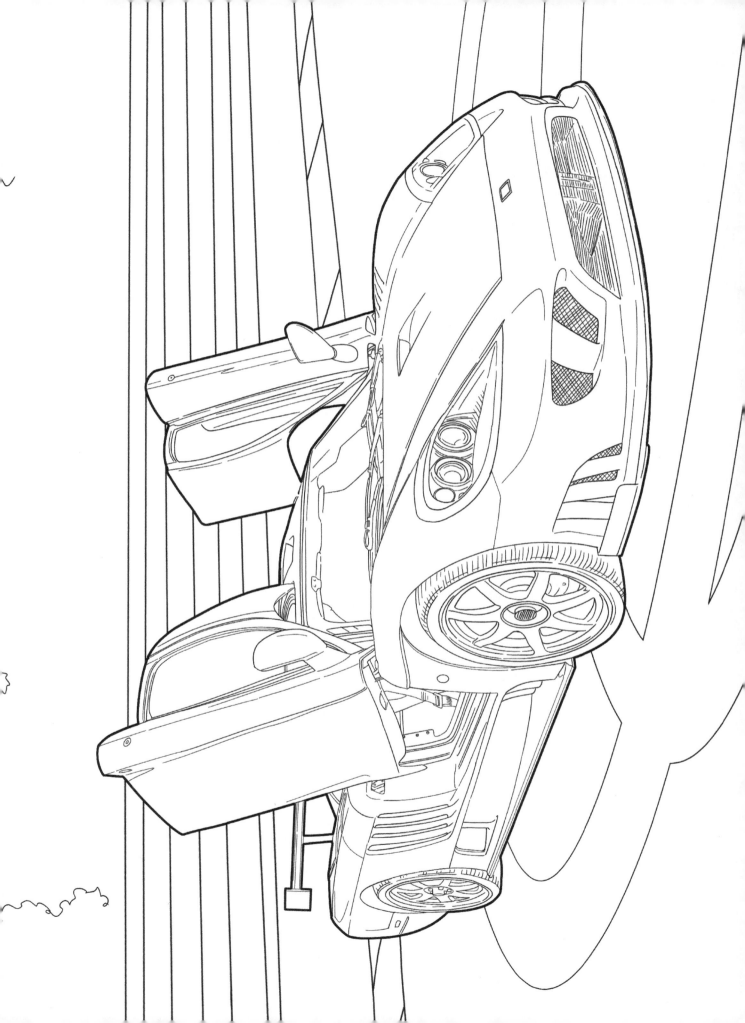

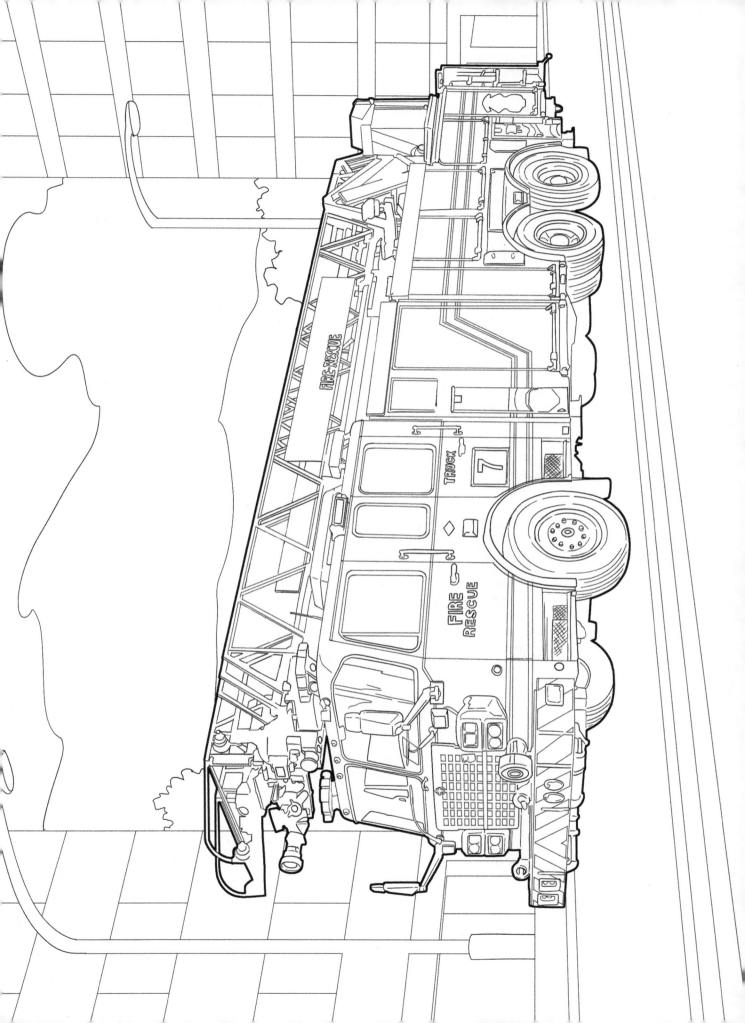

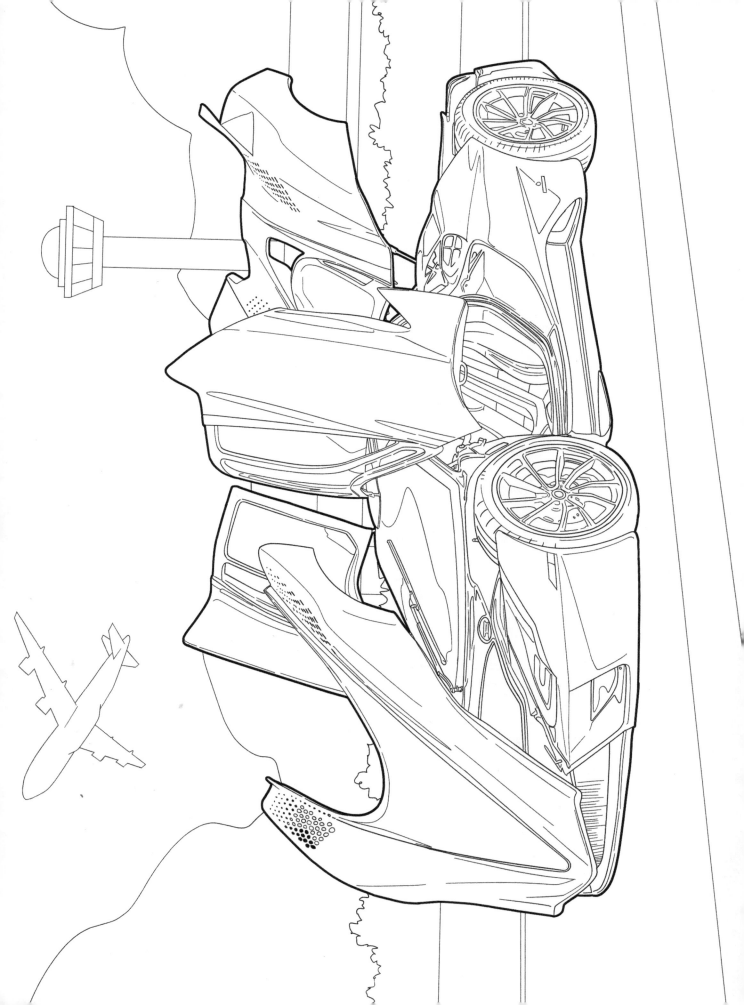